Little Bedtime Journey

Charles J. Ward Jr.

ISBN: 978-0-9988854-4-5

Deepak Chopra, LLC

Together we can help to create a more peaceful, just, sustainable, healthy and joyful world!

October 2, 2017

Charles and Zsuzsanna Ward

Dear Charles,

Thank you for keeping the abundance of the universe circulating in our lives through the sharing of your heartfelt personal journey and gifting me with your first art piece, "Little Bed Time Journey".

It's tremendous to know that you and your daughter are creating a space to reconnect with your "true self — the one without ego, fear or limiting beliefs and a deeper experience of your core being. Congratulations to the both of you!

Wishing you health, happiness, success and wisdom in the field of infinite possibilities.

With warmest regards,

Deepak Chopra

DC:cr

Special Thanks to

Dr. Bernard S. Weinman, Ph. D.,
Professor Allen Koss, Chairman of the Graphic
Design Department, Temple University,
and my wife and children who have inspired me
to write this book.

The art work was created by using pen
and ink drawings, colored pencils, in
combination with original photographs
taken in the Hawaiian Islands.

All concepts, story, and illustrations were
created by
Charles J. Ward, Jr.

Take this book to bed and peek under the covers above your head. You are as happy and healthy as you can be. Get in touch with all your positive energy.

Now into this book you go and when you come out you will know a secret. On your walk down the path collect the tastes of your favorite foods in your mind. You will want them first thing in the morning with the sunshine.

Push through those flowers and vines. We must drink fresh water all the time, so fill yourself up to the brim and if you'd like, go ahead in and clean yourself inside and out. Imagine yourself splashing all about.

You want to continue your journey today but there is a big mountain that stands in your way. To conquer the climb you must go deep inside your mind and find any troubled thoughts that make you frown. Now draw a picture or write the story down. And when you are finished, hand it to me. I will throw it away at the end of this day. You are as light as a feather; you leave some heavy weight behind. Now be on your way and have a good time.

Let's pretend we are standing at the top of a mountain. We can see across the big countryside. What colors can you see? There is a path leading down the mountain. Let's walk down the path. We can get all the way to the bottom in the time it takes us to count backwards from 10 to 1. Not too fast; you can only count each breath as one number. And when you blow each breath out you are blowing away any sadness, any pain, any fears.

10, 9, 8, 7, 6, 5, 4, 3, 2, 1, 0.

All the way at the end of the path, right in front of your eyes, is a tunnel leading downward even more. Now get real comfortable. Close your eyes and see if you can pretend you are riding through a warm yellow tunnel. With your eyes closed let's count down again backwards from 10 to 1, not too fast. Remember you can only count each breath as one number and when you blow each breath out you are blowing away any remaining sadness, any pain, any fears.

10, 9, 8, 7, 6, 5, 4, 3, 2, 1, 0.

When you reach the end of the tunnel, pick your favorite colored balloon and hold it tight, because it wants to float away. There is a soft green hill just waiting for you and your balloon to jump, run, or roll down. If your eyes aren't closed already, close them and see if you can feel yourself going down the soft green hill farther and farther. Down farther and farther all the way to the bottom.

You have traveled a long way down. So just dream for a moment next to the crystal clear water. Put your feet in and feel that the water is not hot nor cold. It is the same temperature that you are. Look in; you can see all the way to the bottom. Pretend the balloon that you are holding is magic and only

in the pages of this book will it give you the magical power to breathe under water.

Now open your hand and let the balloon go higher and higher, getting smaller and smaller, floating into the quiet breeze.

You are already underwater floating in the

light blue colors, slowly drifting down, down

into a rich dark blue, down through a bluish-

purple water,

Deep down into a light purple water, and finally resting on the sandy bottom. The water is hugging you. The sand is so soft as it holds you tightly.

When the water clears there is a treasure chest. You know that inside must be something very important. You turn the key and find the strength to lift the heavy lid.

The treasure comes out of the chest. It is floating all around you. It is filling you up, letting you know that I love you, you are a bright star, a part of this wonderful universe. You have the power to make your dreams come true and shine. All this energy fills your mind and body. It's a present for you to treasure forever.

"Little Bedtime Journey" was created thirty years ago for our children when they were babies, to empower them to believe that they could become any and everything that they dreamed of in life's beautiful journey.

Our oldest son, Charlie Ward always wanted to work in the movie industry. He received his Masters Degree from the American Film Institute/ AFI, worked for Ben Stiller for five years, and now works for Paramount Studios. He has credits in multiple block buster movies.

Our younger son, Adam William Ward always wanted to be an actor. He has expanded his talents to include script writing and film directing. He is successfully following his dreams and is about to release his first full length movie.

Our daughter, Zsuzsanna Eva Ward, better known as ZZ Ward is flourishing. ZZ always dreamed of becoming a professional recording artist. She is now signed to Boardwalk Entertainment and Hollywood Records.

All of our children had a clear vision of what their passions were from a very young age. They stayed focused and have made their dreams come true. "Little Bedtime Journey" was created as an instrument that our children could pick up and read at any time. It has been such an empowering asset in raising our children that we now want to share it with the world.

What are your dreams?

www.ingramcontent.com/pod-product-compliance
Lightning Source LLC
Chambersburg PA
CBHW042019090426
42811CB00015B/1681